JOB-LESS

The Hunt for Sanity

CHRIS BLACKFORD

Published by Jordan Crossing

Cover design and layout by Mullins Creative, Inc.
www.mullinscreative.com

ISBN 978-0-615-40315-1

For my wife, Nicole.

ACKNOWLEDGEMENTS

I'd like to thank Vickie Mullins for helping put all of this together. I don't think I would have gotten this project off the ground without her guidance.

Thanks to Matthew du Mée, Shelley Withem and Melissa Couch for reading my drabble and helping make it into a readable book;

To Mike Withem for helping with the cover design;

And to my wife for letting me write about her and for giving me the support I needed.

FROM THE AUTHOR

Before you begin this book I want to explain a little bit about what you'll find inside. Each chapter is divided into 3 sections: Trial, Lesson, and Challenge.

- *The Trial section highlights the hardships my family and I had during my time of unemployment.*
- *The Lesson section explains what valuable life-lesson I was being taught and how I went about learning it.*
- *And the Challenge section issues you, the reader, a challenge. This takes the lesson talked about in the chapter and gives you suggestions on how to apply it to your life.*

Thanks for your support and I hope you enjoy this book!

Many blessings to you and your family!

~ Chris Blackford

TABLE OF CONTENTS

CHAPTER-ONE

The Sweater Unravels

The feeling is not one to be envied. The dread falls like a half-ton weight, crushing your body beneath with an unrelenting force. Fear washes over you and anger boils underneath your skin. Your income and livelihood have vanished in the blink of an eye. Webster's Dictionary defines *unemployed* as "one who is without a job". Webster apparently was never unemployed. I personally would define being unemployed as: *a terrifying, stressful and uncertain event in a person's life which causes them to question their very sanity.* The statistics we have read about in the paper and on the Internet have now found us; something we didn't think could ever happen. Years of devotion are now shattered upon the rocks. You, like me, suddenly feel like you have just wasted all those years of your life.

When I lost my job it was a new experience for me. The proverbial rug was pulled from under my legs, sending me crashing to the floor. The light at the end of the tunnel was a flashing sign that read "Not An Exit." Maybe you were fired, a result of the struggling economy and a downsizing company. Maybe the entire company folded, leaving you suddenly and unexpectedly on your ear. I've been there. Twice. It is a feeling and a situation that I don't wish on anyone.

Regardless of the method by which you have found yourself on the road of unemployment, I wanted to share with you what I have seen and learned during this time in my life. I don't claim to be an expert on this issue. I am just an average, real life guy who decided to write down the things he has learned while being unemployed. I ask that you join me on this small little trip down this road together. Before this might have looked like a dead end, a road filled with potholes and road hazards. I saw it that way too. However, I hope that by the end of this book, you will come to realize that it is not a hopeless road to be traveled, but one that is filled with valuable lessons for each of us.

The first time I lost my job, I had no warning. Things were going good, at least from what I could tell. I was relatively new, but learning very quickly. I was an estimator for an HVAC company in Arizona. That's Heating, Ventilation and Air Conditioning for those not versed in contractor. I had sent out over $4 million dollars in bids and had received word that we would have at least $250,000 of that as actual jobs. Those of us in the office left on Friday to enjoy our weekends. It had been a productive week and we were hopeful of the future. Saturday, I spent the morning with my wife, enjoying each other's company and talking about an addition we wanted to add to our house. Then my work phone rang. It was my boss calling, which wasn't that unusual, actually. He often worked the weekends and would call me and ask questions or to clarify something I had done. I answered it assuming that it would be for one of those reasons. I remember the words exactly. "Hey Chris. I'm not sure if you heard but I had to shut down the company. I'll need you to come in on Monday and turn in your phone and anything else you might have." That was it. I answered the phone with a job and an optimistic outlook on the future. When I hung up, I was unemployed for the first time in my life.

I laughed when I hung up, a surreal feeling washing over me. "Did that really just happen to me?" I thought out loud. I told my wife and we sat in shock. We had a little savings but only enough for a month of living expenses. I didn't know what to do. I didn't know where to begin to look for another job. I never graduated from college, thus I didn't have a degree to fall back on. I spent most of my life in retail and the HVAC company was the first non-retail job I ever had.

Worst of all, I possessed few marketable skills.

I tried to start where I had left off. Digging for a sense of familiarity, I applied for jobs at other HVAC companies, having learned a lot about the business of commercial HVAC. No such luck. A man with only a few months of HVAC experience was not as hot of a commodity as I had hoped. Reaching for my small bag of connections, I found a man who owned an HVAC company and he went to the same church as my family. I called him and made an appointment to meet with him. I asked him if he was hiring, told him of all that I had just learned, and did my best to impress him with recently learned jargon and fundamentals of AC work. As it turned out, he was only hiring field techs, something I knew nothing about. Regardless of his need at that time, he put me to work in the office and had the hope that I might become a trustworthy long-term employee. It was a hiring out of sheer mercy. I was thankful, nonetheless.

Excited that I had found another job so quickly, I had high hopes about the future and knew I could be a very good employee. Plus, I knew this man fairly well and I liked him. What could be better than working for a man I liked and someone who I genuinely wanted to succeed? I was eager to begin showing my worth.

My hopes for this job quickly died, though. I spent two weeks as a glorified secretary to a man who didn't need one. It was one of the worst experiences of my life. I hate feeling useless and I hate sitting around doing nothing all day. There, I was able to experience both feelings at the same time and became an expert at them both. With a mix of reluctance and relief I left that job and looked for something else. Crazy, I know, given the circumstances.

Using the church connection again, a friend of mine told me to talk to another business owner that went to our church. It was a grading company and I knew nothing about the grading business. I was hired anyway, once again out of mercy. I picked up the job rather quickly, though. Over the next two years I saw this grading business grow slower and slower. I was one of the last office personnel who managed to keep their job, despite the fact I was spending much of the days doing nothing except waiting for the phone to ring. I was once again reduced to being useless and unproductive. Reading the writing on the wall and expecting a layoff to come soon, I spoke with the boss. We agreed that my time had come to an end and that I should be on my way.

Though this was a bit more formal and courteous than a pink slip or a shut down, I was jobless again. This time our savings account was next to empty, as it had been for the two years that I worked for that company. We had moved into a bigger house when my second child was born, which meant a larger mortgage. So with more mouths to feed and larger monthly payments to manage, the pressure of the circumstances started to fall heavily on top of me.

The world economy had taken a nose dive and the unemployment rates were climbing. Before I had left my job at the grading company, I had tried my hand at the real estate market just as the downturn was happening. I refinanced our first home and took out nonexistent equity to buy our new, bigger home. We had sought advice from people we knew and trusted, wanting to make well-informed decisions. However, even they could not have predicted the coming storm in the real estate market. We found renters for our first home, but the rents were not coming close to covering the mortgage. We used the money we pulled out to compensate for the shortage, but the money ran out faster than we had planned. Disciplining ourselves, we were very good about not spending the money on extra luxuries. We did not buy new cars or TVs. No fancy vacation or anything of excess was bought with that money we refinanced. It was used for its intended purpose only.

Despite the precautions we took, we still lost that house to foreclosure. I thought I had done my homework and planned out everything. Clearly I was wrong. That was a gut-retching experience and I was terrified the whole way. I still don't think I am completely out of the woods. Even now, I can feel the fear begin to rise up inside of me, grabbing my stomach with an icy grip.

With no money coming through the door we began struggling to make the mortgage payments on our house. The circumstances squeezed us and we were forced to move, as we had no money, no savings and no income to continue making our payments on that house.

Luckily, we had family close by who knew our circumstance and they opened their home to us, allowing us to move in with them until we could get back on our feet. If my in-laws had not been willing to help us out in that manner, I am not sure what we would have done.

In preparation for the move we sold everything we owned, as much of it as we could let go. Our luxuries in life, though small, were being sold to strangers at rock bottom prices. Our hobbies and personal enjoyments went out the door faster than we could have imagined. I had to call in favors with friends and family to store the things that we did not want to sell. We even had to part with our beloved dog.

Our lives were flipped upside down and there was no end in sight. I could not see any good that could come from this situation and I had to fend off the fear that daily tried to consume me. However, while I battled for sanity and a sense of direction I discovered that I was being taught several valuable lessons about life. These were lessons that I did not know I ever needed to learn. As I turn around and retrace the steps that I have taken over the past months, I can see a common thread that follows my footprints. I was a student of a higher teacher, an instructor that made me his pupil on the subject of life. My life slowly began to change under the instructions of this unknown tutor. Now as I look back I can see that these lessons have helped me maintain my ever elusive sanity during this uncertain time in my life.

I have a feeling that this course that I was unknowingly enrolled in at the beginning of this journey has not been completed. There are many more tests that I must pass before I can graduate to the next level. But I know that I am not the only one who was forced into this school. I know that I am not alone in my search for purpose and direction in a time where the future seems cloudy and bleak. Perhaps you are one of those people, like me, who have lost your job or were forced to move on from your last employer simply because they could not sustain the hours you needed to make ends meet.

Although your circumstances might be slightly different, in essence we are in the same place. Allow me to share with you what I have learned during this time in my life. My desire is that you will find some hope and comfort in these words that I write. This is not because I have an exceptional talent of writing, but because I am a real, flesh and blood person who knows what you are going through. Open your mind and swallow your pride as I share these lessons with you. Some will be hard for you to hear and some you will openly deny that you need to learn them. Believe me, when it came time for me to learn, I went kicking and screaming into the proverbial classroom. While you travel on this rocky, winding road I hope you can find comfort and encouragement in these lessons. You are not alone. We all are in this together.

There is
a Higher Power

TRIAL

Control is one of those feelings that is extremely addicting once you've tasted it. When I am in control of my car, I feel like I can go anywhere I please. Several tons of metal, gas and rubber are under my spell, forced to do what I command it to do. With just a small amount of pressure I can force this machine to fly down the road at incredible speeds. It must turn left or right as I deem fit. When I order it to stop, it responds without an excuse. It is a surreal feeling.

Yet, do I really have all that control? Or is it an illusion of my mind? After all, there are laws that I must follow and police officers to enforce those laws. If I do not obey them I am punished. Other drivers, controlling their own vehicles are on the road as well and I must be wary of them or I could become injured in an accident. My car needs to be maintained for it to function properly and if I neglect repairs or normal upkeep my car will not be in the needed working condition. Weather, malfunctions, gas, oil, other drivers, laws and police officers all come into play when I am driving. I do not have the total control that I think I have. I am confined by the rules of the system. We all are.

There is, however, a power that is beyond the rules of this universe. And when my shortcomings were brought to the forefront of my consciousness, I was forced to acknowledge and submit to the thought and to the understanding that there is a Higher Power out there in the universe somewhere. Whether you believe in God, the Universe, or the Big Cheese, it is imperative that you understand, accept and believe there is someone or something greater than you at work in the cosmos.

For the remainder of this book, I will refer to this Higher Power as God. My personal belief is in God and that is how I will express it for the rest of this book. Before you shut me out and close this book, know that the previous statement is as religious as this book will get. This isn't an overtly religious message nor is it an attempt to convert anyone to any specific way of belief or lifestyle.

While I am unemployed, living with my in-laws

and with no solution in sight, understanding that these things are out of my control has helped me look into the future, knowing God is here with me. He has me traveling this tough road for a reason and the only thing I can control is my response to what is happening. I can choose to be angry and lash out at my family when the stress and fear build to a boiling point. Or I can understand that this is beyond me. I can choose to do my part, but I must leave the outcome to God. I can't make someone hire me. I can't force the economy to turn around and companies to start hiring again.

LESSON

Just like driving, life gives us the illusion that we are in control of what happens to us. We think that we have the ability to move how we wish, where we wish. However, as those of us who are unemployed know, we had little control over what has happened to us. Even if we could go back in time and do something different at our previous employer's business, would that change the outcome of the entire world economy? Sure, if I could go back, I would not refinance my house and take out the equity that was never really there. I would have planned a bit differently how and when I bought my new house. I could give you list after list of things that I would change if I had the option. But I don't have that option and neither do you. What we can do now is move on and learn from the lessons that life has taught us.

When I finally came to the point where I needed to admit and rely on God to help me through this time in my life, many of the pressures that I carried on my shoulders lightened considerably. Shockingly, I was not responsible for making the world turn, for causing the sun to rise or for the changing of the seasons. The world's future is not in my hands, thankfully so. As much as you and I might think it, we are not Superman, charged with the protection and salvation of the planet. Ponder this "new" revelation and truly grasp the impact of ceasing to bear the weight of the world on your back.

CHALLENGE

Pause for a moment before you go any further. Take a day, week or however long it takes for you to decide what it is exactly that you want to believe in. Open your mind to the possibility that you have been misguided if you have not believed in anything up to this point in your life. You may have been wrong before, but I do not want to get into an argument with anyone on this issue. That is not the point of this book. The point is to simply help you acknowledge that this universe is too big and vast to be under our direct control. For us to make it through this life of uncertainty, we must be willing to accept help from a Higher Power, one greater than ourselves.

We were not meant to make it through this unpredictable world all the way through on our own power. It is not a demonstration of weakness to accept and rely on help that is freely available from a Higher Power. Instead it demonstrates great strength and confidence on our part to concede that we need supernatural help. Knowing you need help takes common sense and some humility.

Some things in this life are just beyond our control. What if everything that happens in the universe was put into an equation and we could figure out the actual percentage of control we have? The number would be so small we might as well call it zero. That's right, 0% of the entire universe's actions are under our direct control. We can't help it if our golf game is rained out. You can't control if your son breaks his arm riding his bike or if your friend's cancer returns. The economy, weather, life and death are not our servants. We all are subjects to a greater Master Plan. The most control we can have is a small measure of control over ourselves; our diet, exercise, etc. Most importantly, we can control our *responses* to all the things life throws at us. Including the loss of a job.

You must do your part, do the best you can do and refuse to try to wrestle the control out of God's hands. There is still hope. God is there for you. You have to trust that the things out of your control will work out in the end. Believe that these things are in better hands and that you were not in control of them for a reason. None of us are more qualified than God to handle all these crazy things in our lives.

This is the most important truth that is vital to our success and wellbeing. If we fail to find belief in something greater than ourselves, then the other lessons become much more difficult. Take as much time as you need to learn this lesson and find your belief. The other teachings are all balanced on this one. It's time to believe.

CHAPTER THREE

It's Crowded Here

TRIAL

When problems arise in my life, they often place themselves squarely in my line of sight and grab my undivided attention. Regardless of their true size, my imagination inadvertently feeds them and they grow exponentially until they envelop my mind like a heavy, black tarp. My vision is hindered and I feel like I am in a dark, empty room all alone. "There is no one else," whispers a raspy voice in my head. The voice fills my mind and a fog drapes over my judgment. "You are alone now. Nobody knows how you feel," the voice repeats. I do not have the discernment to tell fact from fiction as the voice continues to fill my head. The feelings of abandonment, depression and anxiety would fall on me like a vicious predator sinking its teeth into helpless prey. Giving up and assuming the fetal position seemed to be the only option that I had left. Hopelessness and fear would pound me mercilessly. I never knew how long these attacks would last or if I would make it through them.

I was ashamed to talk with anyone about my struggles. Embarrassed, I thought I had failed my family and that I was letting everyone down. The realization that I was not strong enough hit me hard and I didn't want anyone else to discover my weaknesses. I thought I was the only one going through this pain and hardship. The suffering that I was going through would manifest itself in my life. Sudden bursts of anger would swell up inside of me, spilling over and crashing into my family, especially my wife and kids. I hated myself during times like this. I knew I was unjustly verbally, emotionally and spiritually attacking them driven by the pain that was inside of me. They did nothing wrong, yet I punished them anyway.

Conversely, if the pain didn't show itself through anger it went the other way completely. Depression and self-pity would consume me and turn me into a weeping, spineless glob of goo. I wanted to curl up in a corner and just die. I convincingly told myself that I did not deserve my circumstances. I had done nothing wrong and none of this was supposed to be happening to me. These manifestations were the loneliest. I hated every minute of them.

LESSON

Then something happened. I am not completely sure what was done or if there was an exact event that opened my eyes but I began to hear about and speak to several people who were in similar situations. People seemed to crawl out of the woodwork to let me know that they were looking for a job or that they were recently laid off. Pastors, friends, acquaintances and strangers told me their stories of unemployment and of their past and present struggles. The uneasiness that I had over living with my in-laws diminished as I heard stories of respected friends, mentors and peers that had gone through or were going through the same living arrangements. I couldn't believe how unnecessary my suffering had been. By shutting my eyes off to the outside world and not seeing what was truly going on around me, I had put myself through so many painful, self-inflicted torture sessions. I was never alone. That realization was a life-saving one for me.

To further prove my point, take a look at the current U.S. unemployment rate. As of right now, it is around 9.7 percent. That means there are about 30 million people who are in the same situation that we are in. That's right; 30,000,000 people (say that number out loud). One out of every ten people we pass on the streets shares our plight. We are, most definitely, *not* alone. We need to understand and accept this truth as soon as we can. The longer we carry the burden of thinking we are alone, the more painful the attacks become and the harder they are to overcome. Do not carry the heavy, painful "loneliness" burden, especially when it is untrue and completely unnecessary. It is a burden none of us have to carry. One none of us *should* carry.

My wife and I try to get together with people as a couple. After all, we are going through this as a family. We have formed lasting friendships with people through this trial in our lives. And good friends are extremely valuable, more than we could ever truly appreciate. They don't run out like the cash in our bank accounts. Their support is the difference between moving on to future success and being stuck in a desperate place for a long time.

CHALLENGE

Do you find yourself succumbing to rage or depression, the feeling of aloneness and self-pity? The first and most important thing is to *know* that you are not alone. Then, do something about it. Find a group who can be there to support you. Ask around at your church, gym or any other social network to find the people who know what you are going through and can be there to support you. Be proactive and find a solid support group to fit yourself into. Get together with friends who are struggling. Encourage each other and bare each other's burdens. Many hands make light work, and the burden of being unemployed is a heavy one. We need all the help we can get!

There is no poison like being alone during this tough time in our lives. Don't listen to the lies the voice inside your head might be saying. Don't let the intimidation and fear blind you to reality. We are never alone, no matter what we are experiencing. Someone has always gone before us. Get connected. Be there to support others as they support you. We all need each other. Together we will make it!

CHAPTER FOUR

HELP: The Other Four Letter Word

TRIAL

Help is an interesting thing for all of us. All of us on this planet have, at some point, struggled with asking for help. Having teeth pulled might be a more desired fate. It doesn't come naturally to any of us. Pride tells us we can do anything. We go out of our way to avoid admitting we need help. Even when we have finally confessed to ourselves that we require assistance, the words painfully slip past our lips to others in the same agonizing way a mother gives birth to a child.

Assistance is not something we want to readily accept. It is not something we ever want to admit we need. Usually, I am not typical when it comes to asking for help. I hate not knowing where I am going, so I always get directions. I am not ashamed to ask. On any shopping experience, my wife adamantly refuses to ask any employee for help to find a specific item. I, however, hate wandering around a store just to find one thing. I want to get in, find what I need and get out. I'll ask every employee I find to point me in the direction of what I am looking for. Why waste my time walking in circles when I can be pointed in the right direction?

That being said, I personally never felt I had a big issue with asking for help. If I know I have a job that will go more smoothly or more quickly with an extra pair of hands, I will find someone who has the appropriate skill set and ask them for help. For example, recently I needed help unhooking a water softener system. And a handyman, I am not. I know how to use a hammer, barely. Knowing I needed help uninstalling it, I made a few phone calls and had a friend come over and help me. After it was unhooked, I had to come back with a truck to transport it. The system was much heavier than I had expected, so I went next door and asked someone who I had never seen before to help me load it into the truck.

With the ease in which I can and do ask for help, I thought this was one lesson that I already knew. Why would I need to learn to receive help when I am not ashamed to ask for it? Yet, there was one particular way I did not like to admit when I needed help: money. I hate asking people for money. Even though the pay checks stopped coming, the bills did not. I had to decide which bills to pay and which bills could wait or, more accurately, would *have* to wait.

Then the holidays came. If there was ever a time when being without income was more demoralizing it was during the Thanksgiving and Christmas holidays. We often didn't have much to spend for those occasions even when I did have a job but our money was running out quickly. I knew there was not much hope of buying anything special for the holidays. It was a reality that we were just going to have to accept.

My wife and I often saw ourselves as people who loved to give. Even when we didn't have much, we still found a way to give the little we had to those who needed it more. We continued to give to our church and other charities. We saw ourselves as the providers and givers to those in need. I don't believe we never truly saw ourselves as one who needed to be the receivers of such gifts.

Thanksgiving passed us by and December was here. We no longer could afford staying in our house and were forced to move in with my in-laws. Talk about a humbling experience. I was used to being the provider. I was the one who paid the bills and brought home the bacon. Now I was unable to provide the simple necessities of life. We moved out of our house and crammed into two 10x10 rooms; one was our bedroom/office/living room and the other my son and daughter's room.

There was once a time when we envisioned being

able to open our home for those who fell upon tough times. We would be the ones who did the rescuing. Never once did we think we would be the ones in the need of a place to stay. How grateful we are to have such a wonderful family. Even now, tears swell in my eyes thinking about how much love they are continue to show me and my family.

Yet the provisions did not stop there. As Christmas approached, we wondered how we could afford gifts for one another and our children. It was breaking our hearts that we couldn't even supply simple presents for our kids. We knew it wasn't about the toys or gifts but the experience of Christmas morning as a family and that is the truth we tried to share with our kids anyway. But we still wanted to have our kids open presents on Christmas morning for the simple joy of watching them do so.

Sometime that same week I received an email from the Youth Pastor at our church. He told us that his high school and junior high kids had "adopted" our family and wanted to provide us with Christmas presents for everyone. And he told me I had little choice in the matter. We tried to talk our way out of this lavish gift, stating that surely there must be another family hurting worse than we were. He told me, "No" was not an acceptable answer.

A few days before Christmas, I headed down to the church office to pick up our gifts. When I got to the church office, I was handed two large bags *full* of Christmas presents for my children from people who had no idea who they were giving to. As I stood holding those bags of gifts, I nearly broke down in tears right then and there. Never before had I experienced anything like that. How blessed we were to receive this love poured out upon us. We were so thankful. My children had something to open on Christmas morning all because people gave. Even though this was one of the hardest times in our lives, it was the best Christmas I can remember. I will never forget this Christmas.

The Christmas gifts and moving in with my in-laws are the main examples of how I was taught to receive help. There were other times when blessings would show up on our doorstep. Cash would arrive in the mail in an unmarked envelope. Gift cards were delivered to us from various sources, providing what we needed to purchase groceries. Our cell phone bill was picked up as a Christmas gift and our children received clothes they needed. We also received a Thanksgiving basket, full of the traditional food items served for that holiday.

LESSON

Receiving help is an amazing thing to learn. You might think this is an attribute we would not have difficulty in learning. After all, most of us love to get gifts on our birthday or Christmas or any other day. There is not a woman in the world who would not love to get flowers or little tokens "just because". But these are rarely, if ever, gifts we *need*. They do not come when we are in a desperate situation. They often are traditional, things we do year after year. Like turkey on Thanksgiving, you get gifts on your birthday.

The willingness to receive presents for an occasion requires little humility and they are often anticipated, if not expected. The gifts and help that I needed to learn to receive could also be translated as *charity*. Does that word make your cringe? Especially if you know you are the one receiving that charity? It takes humility to accept charitable giving from others. And humility is not a natural characteristic we possess.

CHALLENGE

This is the hardest, longest lasting lesson any of us will ever have to learn. It doesn't matter what stage of life you are in, humility is a lifelong teacher, often forcing curriculum down our throats. And we kick and scream, fighting every inch along the way. But it is a lesson we *must* learn. If we fail to heed its teachings, humility will flunk us and force us to retake the whole course again. It's like Algebra I; we have to take it until we pass and once we do, Algebra II is what we have to look forward to. However, once we become obedient to the lessons of humility, all the other lessons it has to teach us will simply build upon that which we already learned. It won't become easier but we will be more susceptible to humility's leading. And unlike Algebra, this is a lesson we won't soon forget.

We should not try to trudge through this tough time alone, trying to muscle, drink, fight, or smart our way out. People want to help us. Sometimes the help will come without us asking for it. Don't ignore it or fight it. Other times, we need to ask. There is no shame in asking for help, we all need it sometimes. It takes more courage to admit and seek help or charity than it does to play tough while we crumble on the inside. We were not meant to walk this road alone. There is no reason for us to start now.

CHAPTER FIVE

Learning True Priorities

TRIAL

Over the years I can remember making several lists that contained my priorities in numeric order. God was always the first, followed by family, then friends. Work came after that with hobbies and whatever else was a part of my life in that particular season. I'm sure that you had or currently have a list that is similar to mine. It would not surprise me to learn that most of us share three of the top five things on our priorities lists. We all know in our minds how important God, families and friends are to us. Our work, since we spend most of our time there, makes the list too. After all, we have to care about our work. Even if we are not employed it will most likely still make it into the top five.

I do not ever remember having a tangible possession on my list. My cars, toys, collectibles or personal items were never seemingly important enough to me to have them on my lists. Never had I thought that those things could be or should be more important than friends, family, work or God. Why should they be? Most of the things I own now or had owned in the past were all things that could be replaced. But how could I replace my wife or my kids? My brothers and sisters or parents? Would we ever want to replace our true friends with things? So why did I often live as though my stuff was more important to me than anything else?

I remember working for a convenience store chain called QuikTrip. It was a gas station by any other name but the company was a solid one and it bucked the stereotypical gas station stigma that other chains had. Case in point: my wife would prefer to only use their restrooms if the need arose while out and about.

I was working in the northern part of the city in which I live and that translated into a richer class of people. I would see nice cars all day long driven by sharply dressed people who seemed busy with the lifestyle of the wealthy. One regular client, for example, played football for the Buffalo Bills when they were the AFC champions in the 90's.

I watched these lives from afar for over a year. A deep feeling began festering inside me that longed to have what they had. I wanted the fancy cars with the bank accounts to match. I wasn't particularly happy at my job and seeing these people flaunt the success I presumed they had began to infect me. I was barely making it even though I was paid considerably well despite being so young with no college education. I never thought I would care so much about the stuff in life that I did not have.

Now I find myself even further from the level of wealth and possessions that I had envied a few years ago working at that gas station. Although I have moved past the envious desires that I had back then, the temptation to place things – *stuff* – higher on my priorities list is still there. I often don't notice their rise in status until I am forced to part with that which has moved up the list, whatever that may have been. It became a flashing sign, a blaring alarm in my life when the true value that I had placed on these things was revealed to me. It was convicting knowing the self-proclaimed important things in my life (God, family, friends, etc.) were somehow surpassed by inanimate objects.

My wife wanted me to include a "case-in-point" here and I fought to not include the example she had readily at hand. After thinking about it, I reluctantly agree that it is a fair example. When we first were married I had recently discovered the online gaming craze. I have always been a gamer but was hesitant to join the online crowd. However, with newly installed upgrades on my computer and a high speed internet connection, I became an "online gamer". I was hooked. I played every spare minute I could. I even played the minutes I could *not* spare. It was consuming all the time my wife needed. One day she couldn't take it anymore. She blew up! I do not remember the exact threats she made *to the computer* but I do remember they were illogical and silly. She started the ranting boiling with anger and it ended with both of us laughing. Her point, however, was made and I have tamed that addiction.

When I lost my job, my true priorities were put to the test. This wasn't so much of a teaching time as it was a pass/fail trial by fire. I had to learn quickly what was meaningful to me, and what I could live without. Desperation began to seep into our minds and lives and my wife and I decided that we needed to sell some of our things to try to make ends meet for a little longer. We had very little savings when I was working full time and when I lost the steady paycheck that my job supplied, the money that we did have was not going to last. We were praying that things would quickly change and that the numbers in our bank accounts would not matter.

Things did not change quickly enough. Going though our home with a fine toothed comb, we inventoried everything. I mean we emptied closets, the garage, everything trying to find things we could sell. We started simple, finding things that were collecting dust in corners and buried deep in closets. Things we had forgot we had or things we did not need anymore. A sewing machine here, golf clubs there. A Total Gym and my Xbox made the list along with a deep freezer, some baby toys and other random furniture we didn't need. Surprisingly, those things sold fairly quickly. We still were coming up short, however.

Soon we found ourselves taking an even more careful and thoughtful approach to the things in our house. What could we buy again, when the time came? What was irreplaceable? What things would we lose forever if we sold them? There were handmade toy chests and antique tables and other items that had sentimental value to us that we knew we would have not been able to buy again if we sold them. When our house was on the line, we found out quickly what we really did need and what was just extra.

After we gathered our inventory, made our lists and posted things online, we planned a garage sale for the next few weekends. Against our secret desires and sooner than we expected, people began buying our stuff. The prices quickly dropped lower and lower. Our things, our stuff, our treasures were being sold at rock bottom prices. It was like having my guts ripped out and trampled on. We spent hours sitting in silence, my wife and I, just reflecting on all of our things that were suddenly gone forever. It wasn't so much that we sold things that had great value or were especially unique. But all of it was *ours*.

We had lived a simple life and we did not have a lot of stuff before the sale. We went without many of the things most people would have considered normal. We had a hand-me-down TV, nothing fancy or big. We had a hand-me-down couch and recliner and an armchair we picked up from someone's yard. Almost everything in our house was a hand-me-down or something we picked up for free. The pain still came though when we sold those items. We did not live in excess yet we were being forced to give up what we did have.

LESSON

This required us to consider all that we had and prioritize it to the nth degree. This was the hardest lesson for me personally. I felt like I was being punished. I remember the day when my wife and I sold several items in one day. Tears would come and go and we would alternate in the role of comforter. That's how the days would go. One of us would be wallowing in despair and regret and pain. The other would reach out to lift the one hurting. We made it through those first few tragic days, one step at a time.

It was painful to see our stuff leave. The pain lessened over time, thankfully. As the sharp stabs of grief and regret began to dull, I began to see how truly blessed we were to be able to have those things in the first place. Plus, I knew we still had plenty for which we could give thanks. We still had our families who were there to support us. We had our health, which was an extra blessing because we did not have health insurance. We had our friends, who told us we were in their prayers and gave us the support we needed. We discovered that even though we didn't have much, we could still slim down and still live a very blessed life.

When all else is stripped away, we begin to see the true value in what we already have. Through somber eyes we will see what our true needs are and what was extra. In a society that forces the idea of "consume, consume, consume" this lesson flies in the face of all that we are inundated with everyday. The car companies, credit cards and retail stores hypnotize us into thinking that we are not going to be happy or satisfied unless we have a new car in the driveway, a credit card in our wallet and a 60" plasma TV in the living room.

Do we really need to buy a new car when our old one goes over 50,000 miles? Is the latest techno gizmo really vital to our existence? Can we really afford to charge now and pay later? How has that worked out for us so far? We are very spoiled in our lives today, with the latest and greatest available to us at competitive prices at almost every store on every corner. Honestly, I want new cars and a bigger TV. I'd love to get all the latest technology gizmos. But, do I *need* those things to make me happy? Will they make my life complete? Would I only be satisfied if I had a big TV or luxury SUV? The answer is an emphatic, "No!"

It is important to recognize the true priorities in our lives. This lesson should be learned now, when times are tough. We will have a greater appreciation for those things in life that we had taken for granted previously. And what a great lesson we can teach our kids, to be content with what they have and not long for things they will only get bored with a few weeks later. They will carry that lesson with them for a long, long time. Find your true priorities in this life during this season. It will strengthen us as people and as a family if we do.

CHALLENGE

I challenge you to make a *new* list. Prioritize the things in your life that are most important to you and your family. Then I challenge you to *live* by that list. Now is the greatest opportunity you have to rearrange your life and to make those things the most essential. The things in my life that had inadvertently become most important to me were stripped away from my tightly clinched hand. What remained were those things which no one could take from me. My God would never leave me and no one could steal my faith. My family remained beside me even though the times were uncertain and the road was rocky. My eyes were opened. I saw that I could survive without those things I once held so dear. Those things were fleeting. But my *true* priorities remained. This is a tough and somber thing to learn, but it is important. If you realize now that you had been living your life with messed up priorities, don't wallow in self-pity. We have all made mistakes and we all have switched around those things in our lives. Don't dwell on the past but decide today to live a new life. Use this fresh start to find what matters most to you. Then live that out in your life today.

CHAPTER SIX

Take the Time

TRIAL

Time is something we all have, that we are all endowed with at the moment of our birth. We all have the same 24 hours in a single day. No one has the ability to add to his sum, no matter what skills or education he possesses. Time is often spoken in terms most commonly used for currency. We can invest it wisely or waste it foolishly. It can be spent vigorously or saved conservatively. We have either too much or not enough. We can lose track of it unintentionally or purposefully be over conscious of it. We can give it freely or be stingy with it.

Time is a precious commodity, and unlike money, once it is spent or lost it can never been gained again.

Benjamin Franklin said once that "Lost time is never found again," and that truth became more real to me when I began to have time to spare. I am not constrained to a schedule or tied down by a time clock at this time in my life. I no longer have to carve out a portion of my day to spend in an office somewhere. I now have all the time in the world.

When I worked for QuikTrip, the gas station, my schedule had me working the 3rd shift, the overnight, for about a year. I begged and pleaded to be moved to a different shift so that I could actually be on the same living cycle as everyone else I knew. I never saw any of my friends or family simply because I was on the opposite sleeping rotation. The upper management finally obliged and changed my schedule. And then they changed it again. And again. It changed so much that I worked every major and minor holiday for the three years straight. While everyone I knew was enjoying a day off to spend with their families on Thanksgiving, eating turkey and mashed potatoes, I was at work with strangers choking down a hot dog and chips. While the entire United States was at home opening present on Christmas morning, I was mopping floors and cleaning public restrooms. For three years I spent Christmas and Thanksgiving and every other holiday in my work uniform. New Year's Eve and Day were not reasons for me to celebrate. Labor Day, Memorial Day, Veterans Day, Presidents Day and Independence Day were just another day at the office for me while my friends had parties and enjoyed each other's company. It was miserable.

When I finally was able to leave that job, I traded the weird and intrusive times for longer weekdays and take-home work. The scheduled and promised forty hours grew to 50 or more. I was always exhausted. I did not have the energy to spend significant time with my kids, my wife, or my friends. I missed them terribly and my wife often complained, justifiably so, about our time together. My kids missed me, often waking up in the morning and asking where I was. This was not the life I wanted to have, but it was the one I had out of necessity. After all, I had bills to pay.

LESSON

Then unemployment came. The once early mornings and late evenings vanished and were replaced by hours of free time. I no longer had to work late into the evenings. My alarm clock had no reason to scream at me to get out of bed. I have been able to sleep more during this time than I can ever remember. I did not, for your information, become incredibly lazy. I still wake up relatively early in the morning, almost never getting past 7:30 AM. However, that is a far cry from 5 AM. The difference in how rested I feel is astounding!

I also had the opportunity to share lots of time with my family. Honestly, I once cringed at the idea of spending all day with my kids. I anticipated being driven to the brink of insanity. Although they have their moments of pushing me beyond my limits psychologically, I have been able enjoy massive amounts of time being their father. It is a role in today's society that often falls by the way side, seen as a less important role than the mother. Being a father is more than working countless hours. I discovered and learned more about what it meant to truly care for and love my children. We would spent hours playing games with each other and going to the park. Grocery shopping and household chores became special bonding times that we enjoyed together. I get to read to them more and I've been able to see my son develop as a reader and a writer. My daughter even calls for Daddy more often than Mommy now, much to my wife's chagrin.

Besides being around to watch and enjoy my children, my wife and I have been able to invest our time with each other more as well. We have experienced more intimate, meaningful time together than we ever have before. We share the things we are learning and are struggling with and lift each other up when we need it. We pray more and we spend our evenings reading books we both enjoy. We are closer now than we have ever been. This is priceless to me, well worth any cost I must pay.

This change has been a welcome one in my life. Things have been tough; I won't deny that. There are days when I want to break down and give up. We have had to make some big decisions, ones I would not like to make again. We had to give up a lot of things that we held dear. We have sacrificed greatly and it was a painful transition. The struggles are not over yet and I anticipate that there will more tough days ahead.

The losses we have suffered are nothing, however, to what we have gained. I know that when I am on my death bed, as my family gathers around me, none of my kids will say they wished they had more toys when they were younger. They won't say they wished I had made more money so we could buy them more stuff. Their memories won't be filled with all the things that I was able to buy them over the years. Their minds, instead, will be flooded with precious memories of our time together. They'll cherish the times we laughed together and the times we cried together. Long after I am gone, it is their memories of the things we did as a family that they will treasure forever. My wife and I have made this a time we will cherish forever. We gave up material possessions to gain things we could not buy.

My friendships have also benefitted from my time away from work. I have had the time to hang out and fellowship with my dearest friends. New relationships have been given the opportunity to develop and grow into more meaningful, powerful bonds. My wife and I have been able to join others for fun and companionship. Before I lost my job, we would struggle to have any type of meaningful friendships. We would be unavailable to cultivate any relationships with others. We both began to feel that void in our lives, like a black hole deep inside us that consumed our passion for life. The lack of close friends within our social circle was more devastating than we knew. Now, however, we have new flourishing friendships and existing ones are deepening with every week that passes. We purposefully leave slots in our schedule to fill with activities with those precious people we love to spend time with.

CHALLENGE

Even though the stress is high and the money is tight right now in our lives, we need to use this time to spend with our families and friends. I have the pleasure of living in the same state as all my brothers and sisters. The time that I get to spend with them is priceless. If you can, go see your siblings and your parents. Get to know them better now that you have some time on your hands. Try to find out if there is anything you can do for them while you are not confined to a schedule or restricted by a time clock. I have made myself available to my family to help them if they are in need. For example, I've been able to help my dad with work around the house after he had severe back pain. I was glad was able to be there and help him out after all he had done for me over the years.

Be extra sensitive with your spouse, knowing that financial hard times is the top reason for people to end their marriages. The stress will weigh heavily on you both and that extra burden will take its toll. Be mindful of what you say. Your words to your spouse under great stress can carry extra poison if not kept in check. You can unintentionally hurt each other and that only adds to the anger and pain you are feeling. You are in this together; don't make an enemy where a friend currently exists. Instead, be diligent to speak to each other in words of encouragement, even if, no, especially when you don't feel like it. Your situation is no one's fault, so don't direct your frustration at the ones you love.

If you are a spouse of the person who lost their job, you have a vital role in the life of your partner. Watch your words and actions around them. For you wives, it is especially important for you to understand the crushing weight that your husband has upon him now. Go out of your way to encourage him. Don't put more pressure on him by blaming him for things that are not his fault. If he struggles with motivation, don't harshly push him into action, but build him up and send him out. Like a general who rallies his troops before a battle, so you must be that kind of motivation for him. Understand that he will respond better to your signs of respect than to your nagging or judgment. Show him that despite his lack of income you still respect his leadership and responsibilities, that he is still "The Man". And if you work, don't hold that over his head. Don't rub it in.

To both of you, remember to still find time to enjoy each other's company. Get out and go for walks in the park or picnics. Date each other. Love each other. Inspire each other. Cry with each other. Be intimate with each other. After all, you're unemployed, not dead. Get away for a bit if the pressures begin to crush you. Go camping or hiking. There's no need to spend lots of money to do so. Just make it a point to still enjoy life with your beloved.

Take notice too, that your kids are watching you and how you treat each other in the worst of times. Show them what marriage is about now. They will take those lessons with them into their relationships when they are older. Some of the most powerful things we can teach our kids are often the things we don't know we are teaching them.

Some of you don't have spouses or children to spend time with but you do struggle to find, grow and successfully maintain good, healthy friendships. You are lost when it comes to finding good friends. I used to, and still do struggle with, making friends quickly. But, like everything else that holds meaning to us, finding and maintaining quality friendships takes work. We have to be willing to understand that most people wait for others to come to them. Rarely do people take the initiative anymore. If you know that you have a hard time with this, you must grasp that the friendship road is a two way street. Both parties must contribute. But often all it takes is a small push to get the ball rolling. Step up and make that first push when it comes to creating a new friendship.

As to where to begin your quality friendship, I'd recommend looking in the places you spend the most time. Your church or gym or sports clubs that you belong to. Even Facebook has its uses here. Perhaps you even have a lot of informal acquaintances, people who know you but you wouldn't classify them as friends. We had such a couple in our lives. We knew them and they knew us. We never talked more than once a week at church; even then it was merely a courteous greeting. Then one day, I had the urge to simply say, "Hey, we are looking for friends." What was their response? "Cool! So are we!" Now, they are some of our closest friends. It can be as simple as that. Just be willing to take that first step.

None of this quality time happened when I worked a full time job. I was up too early and home too late to have any meaningful time to spend with my family or friends. The weekends were spent catching up on the neglected house work. We were also very involved with our church and spent most of the day Sunday volunteering there. That usually felt more like a half day of work than a true day off. Thus, my schedule was rarely open and I did not have the will power to add anything more to it.

Remember, jobs change but family lasts forever. Don't let this opportunity to build these vital relationships in the midst of these hardships pass you by. If you take the time today, your family will be more prepared to take on any challenges that await you later in this life. These are the times when the bonds are strengthened between our families. They harden to form an unbreakable tie that weaves you and your family together. Don't forsake these relationships. If our families fall apart during this time, we have a greater chance of collapsing under the weight and losing this battle on every front.

Our lives will not be remembered by what job we had or how much money we made. Our legacy is not about what car we drove or how many of them we owned. Our legacy is our family and friends and the impact we had on their lives. Take special time to be with the ones you love the most. Our families do need us to provide for them. But they need us to be the fathers or husband first. Being a good daughter or son, or an attentive mother or father has a longer lasting effect than any job title we might have. Take a break from this busy life we all have and be a better friend, parent or spouse. You will be gaining something that no amount of money could ever buy.

Time is a precious thing. Don't waste it. Focus on the here and now with your family and the job situation will work itself out. We should do what we need to do, but we should not get lost in the process or the stress. If we neglect each other during this rough time, we'll find ourselves in a miserable place in our lives once the storms have past. There will be no one left to help us keep our ships afloat. Let us invest the time we have in the people we love the most. The dividends that will be paid back to us are immeasurable.

CHAPTER SEVEN

Learn to Count ...
Your Blessings

TRIAL

What does it mean to be blessed? You can ask a hundred people what it means to them and you will probably receive a hundred different answers. Is it a blessing to have wealth or a fancy car? Is it enough to have an amazing body or the perfect hair? Is just being alive a blessing? Do we have the things that we would consider blessings? Or are they something we long for? At any point in our lives it can be hard to consider ourselves blessed. When times are hard and things seem to be spiraling out of control, it becomes increasingly difficult to count those blessings.

It was hard for me to look past what I was losing when our stuff was seemingly being sold to the lowest bidder. I was so focused on what I was losing that I failed to see the things that could never be taken from me. The importance of family has already been mentioned but it cannot be restated enough. No one can take my family from me. We were all healthy. We still had our friends and our church. No one could foreclose on our faith or belief that God had something planned for us. We had a place to live even when we lost our house. We had extended family that supported us and were there to help us in any way they could. Friends at church encouraged us and lifted us up in prayer and none of them looked down at us. Nothing could take these precious things from us.

When we are faced with tough obstacles, we often become consumed with fear. We are scared about what we might lose. We decide that if we had more of this or some of that, our lives would somehow right themselves and we could continue on. These thoughts obscure our mind like a thick fog. Our focus is disrupted and our vision blurred. The trials take our minds captive and we easily forget what we still have, and what we can never lose.

LESSON

We, as a family, have spent more time with close friends in the past 6 months than we had ever in the years past, probably combined. Our relationships with our family grew stronger as we were living in the same house as my wife's mom and step-dad. When we moved in with my in-laws, my wife and I both thought the tension would be thick and the disagreements would be plentiful. Conversely, they have yet to exist. I was available to help with yard work when my dad couldn't physically do it. I was able to watch over my nephew when there were doctors' appointments and no one else was available because of their work schedules. Had I been restricted by a boss or a schedule I would have not been able to do those things.

It is sometimes a difficult practice but I try to find different things that I can be thankful for during this uncertain time in my life. For example, one discovery by accident is that I have lost weight. People just kept telling me that I looked thinner so I had to find out for myself. I don't know why it took a job loss for me to drop 20 pounds, but I guess I'll take whatever I can get!

CHALLENGE

Start a list of things that you can be thankful for. Make it an assignment for you and your family. This will help you take your eyes off the crashing waves. It will drive your focus to the things in life that you are blessed to have. Take time right now to write down at least three things for which you are grateful. Post them on your mirror or in your car. Make your list the background on your computer or on the screensaver. Put it somewhere you will see it every day. Allow it to be a reminder to yourself of all that you have. Don't let the failures and disappointments of the job search consume you. This is a vital step in keeping your sanity as the question marks remain in your future.

Understanding what it means to be blessed is a harrowing task. We should not take this lesson lightly as we move forward during this turbulent time in our lives. It is a crucial step in bringing us to a place of humility and thankfulness, two cornerstones in rebuilding our lives. Each of us will have a different definition of what blessed means to us. But make no mistake, we *are blessed*.

CHAPTER EIGHT

When You Have Nothing Left, Give

TRIAL

By all noticeable accounts, the day seemed to be like any other. The work day had just about come to its conclusion and people started to head home for the day. The streets were packed with the rush hour crowds. Happy hour was minutes away and people were anxiously awaiting the chance to ease into their evenings with a few colds ones with their friends. Then, at 4:53pm local time, their world changed. The earthquake was a catastrophic 7.0 magnitude. Buildings crumbled as the ground shook violently. Screams could be heard as concrete and metal twisted and crashed to the earth. The ground was stained with blood as the death toll reached 230,000 people. An estimated 300,000 more were injured, scrambling to get aide in any way they could. Over a million people no longer had homes to return to.

The devastating earthquake in Haiti is still fresh on everyone's mind. Months later, many continue to struggle to get basic necessities such as clean water, food and medical help. Countless numbers of children are now orphans, their families buried deep under crushed cities and towns. When the news broke of the desolation that Haiti had suffered, America took the lead as it always does it the midst of a world catastrophe and began flooding the country with aid. Money, supplies, volunteers and rescue workers began pouring out of countries around the world to aide in the rescue mission. As a country, we responded with vigor to offer our help.

The world, more specifically America, is in one of the toughest financial times in recent history. Yet as word of another country's suffering reached our shores we looked past our personal struggles and reached out with helping hands to those in need. Though our pocket books are lighter and our bank accounts smaller than we can remember, we still put aside our personal struggles to aide those in dire need. This is one of the many reasons I will *never* be ashamed to call myself an American!

LESSON

The people of Haiti are suffering tragically, but we can look into our own culture, our own hometowns and backyards, and see that there are people who are hurting as well. We are not the only ones struggling to make ends meet. Families have to decide every day which bills they can pay and which will move to collections. Knowing that some families have to decide between electricity and food breaks my heart. I cannot fathom having to make decisions like those. When things like this are brought to my attention, I know that although my circumstances are difficult I am in far better shape than many people out there right now. That is one of the reasons I cannot stop giving.

When things begin to get tough regarding our bank accounts, it becomes increasingly difficult to continue charitable giving. That is the one area where most people see as optional, the least vital part of our budgets. When incomes shrink, giving tends to be the first area people cut back. Honestly, I can't say I really blame them. Our problems rise above our heads and consume our attention and focus. We center ourselves on solving our own issues and subconsciously we slip into the space between "giving" and "needs charity". We slide into a place where we cannot continue to give yet we are still not quite ready to admit we need donations. But we *must* not stop our donations to those in need.

There is a story in the Bible that emphasizes this point. A poor widow came to the temple and she gave a few small copper coins to the needy. As she passed by, a few rich men came behind her and gave bags and bags of gold. Jesus, who watched this process, turned to his followers and shared a significant truth with them. He said that the woman who gave the pennies gave far more than the rich who gave the gold. He said, "For they all contributed out of their abundance, but she out of her poverty put in all she had to live on." (Luke 21:1-4) It cost her greatly, yet she still saw the importance of continuing her giving. She gave even though she would have been considered by most as the one in need. That's heroic!

CHALLENGE

Take a lesson from a single mother from long ago; even when you have little to give, give anyway. God will smile down on you and be pleased by your compassion. You will achieve a greater sense of appreciation for all that you have. You will learn an invaluable lesson and pass this lesson on to your kids. Teaching your kids to be compassionate and caring even when they have their own problems will prepare them to grow up and be men and women who will change the world.

Be courageous and continue your giving even when it hurts. It will be hard, a constant struggle to write those checks to our charities or churches. But we must see past our own pain and hardships to see that there are still those who are in great need. We cannot risk assuming someone else will pick up our mantle and carry it for us. That 'someone' might not ever show up. We need each other to make it through every day of this unpredictable and tough world we live in. This planet turns on the generosity of those who give. If we stop giving back to our communities, this world would suffer a terrible loss that we would not recover from. Be heroic and make that sacrifice for those suffering around you. Our little gifts make a big difference in the lives of others. Whether you give to an organized charity or church or whether you find someone on the street that needs a hot meal, make the brave choice like the widow did. Don't stop your giving. Make a difference in someone's life today.

Dare to Dream

TRIAL

It all starts with a dream. Everything you see started as a dream in someone's head. The United States began as a dream in the minds of a few brave men who dared to pursue them regardless of the result. Thomas Edison *failed* a thousand times to create the light bulb but he did not let his dream die. Henry Ford received a pocket watch when he was a young boy and he immediately became fascinated by the mechanics. This fascination grew into an obsession and he went on to build one of the greatest business empires the world has ever seen.

These men, in their own way, did what was necessary to make their dreams a reality. Regardless of how fierce the opposition was, they refused to give up. Their dreams were powerful. These men *dared* to dream big! They refused to let the antagonists keep them from achieving their aspirations. And they changed the world. Our dreams are equally as powerful. Our dreams have the ability to change our world if we only have the courage to pursue them.

I heard somewhere that 80 percent of the men in the U.S. hate their jobs. Isn't that astounding? That means 8 out of every 10 men you pass on the streets hates their occupation. No wonder road rage is such a problem! Not only do people get stuck in burdensome traffic, but they do so while going to and from a job that boils their blood! Why would these men suffer at a job they abhor? It's shockingly simple really—they have bills to pay. They go to work every day even though they hate every minute of it because they have to. They gave up any dreams they once had to cash consistent paychecks.

Was this you in your last job? Did you *hate* your job? I remember those long drives to work. Secretly, I was hoping to be in a car accident so I wouldn't have to spend of a few days at that place. I would rather have been in that hospital bed than at my desk or in my uniform. Can you relate? Does this describe your last job? For me, it describes most of my working experience. I have yet to have a job that I remotely liked, let alone loved. I surrendered all that I dreamed of doing for the meager pay check. After all, I had bills to pay.

Why do we sacrifice our dreams for those bank deposits? Can we really put a price on our dreams? Then why do we? Maybe you gave up on your ambitions for a pay check too.

LESSON

Now we find ourselves in a place that might be the best chance to pursue those dreams we let slip away. Maybe you have always wanted to go into business for yourself, create a company that you could pour your heart and soul into. Perhaps you've always wanted to try your hand at a special profession, one that you have been drawn to for many years. Don't let your dreams and desires pass by again. Strive harder after them and make them a reality in your life. Do not let fear detour you or the temptations for that paycheck lure you away. God gave you those dreams for a reason. Act now to finally pursue them. If you have the courage to chase your dreams God will support you and provide a way for that to happen.

Be careful though, if you start to strive after those dreams of yours you will have opposition all around you. They say misery loves company and they are right. The 80% of men that hate their jobs have experienced the death of their dreams and the last thing they want is to see someone else living their own. But misery is a terrible companion and a real party pooper. A fulfilled life, however, is calling you away from the 80 percent into the 20 percent. Being miserable often comes to us naturally. It is the easier way to go when the decision comes to follow your dreams or take the "safer" route. Following our own dreams requires courage and that makes the decision much harder. Don't take the easy way this time, friend. You were made for so much more than that.

CHALLENGE

What are your dreams? Are you living them out? Or are they buried deep within your consciousness? Do you dare to take them out only when you are alone, not willing to risk another seeing that which you hold most dear? Are your dreams still alive? Are they dead? Take time now to assess the status of your dreams. Dig them out from the back recesses of your mind. Remember why they were special to you.

When someone is living their dream, their life radiates an energy that hypnotizes others around them. It fills them with electricity that often stays with them for a long time. Why can't this radiant life-giving energy be coming from you? Do not let your dreams die. If they are dead, resurrect them now! This is a perfect time for you to pursue them. See this time as a God-send, a news flash, strongly urging you to pick up your dreams and run with them. Fear, doubt and the miserable people around you will do anything to keep you from chasing those dreams. Do not let them win.

Before you begin to pursue your dreams, however, let me make sure you understand what I am *not* saying. I am *not* saying abandon everything to chase your dreams. We all have responsibilities now that we *must* take into account. If you are a twenty-something single person with no one dependent upon you, you are obviously in a stronger place to chase whatever it is that you want. Conversely, if you are middle-aged with a family to support and a mother-in-law who is living with you in her ending years, you have an obligation to maintain that responsibility. I am definitely not giving you permission or approval to ditch those who are looking to you for support to pursue a dream. I don't want you to give up on that dream, but you must take a realistic and humble look at your life with your loved ones. Decide together if it is feasible for you to pursue those dreams at this stage in your life.

My family is a great example of this. I have a brother-in-law whose dream it is to become a fireman. He is doing everything he can to make this dream of his a reality. Yet he still is providing for his wife by working another job until he is hired by a city as a full time fireman. I also have a brother who loves working with kids. His dream is to coach soccer and he does this every season.

I also have family members who are on the other end of the spectrum. My oldest brother wants to play golf professionally. He is very good too. However, he has a family to provide for and to pursue this dream of his full time would put a lot of that at risk financially. He knows this. He has not given up on this dream entirely, but he knows right now is not the time for him to drop everything and move whole-heartedly towards this goal.

I hope you understand my point of taking into consideration all that you have in your life right now and making an informed, wise decision about your dreams and your future. Do not give up on those dreams of yours, just don't pursue them with carelessness and reckless abandonment either.

Walt Disney took a love for drawing and turned it into the greatest empires known worldwide. Mickey Mouse, a character Disney was forced to create after his first popular character was underhandedly stolen from him, is the most known and loved character worldwide. Walt Disney pursued his dreams whole-heartedly. Steve Jobs and Bill Gates are two men who radically changed the technology arena with the invention of the personal computer. You cannot go through your daily life without encountering a piece of technology that doesn't have their names written all over them. Alexander the Great wanted the world. He settled for nothing less. There will be people who tell us it is impossible to achieve our goals. Impossible, however, is not a word. It is just a reason for people not to try. Dare to dream, my friend, but remember to dream responsibly. Dream big and make it happen!

CHAPTER TEN

Stand Firm, Fear is Coming

TRIAL

During World War II the 82nd Airborne Division became possibly the most well known and honored set of men in the United States Armed Forces. When the missions were hopelessly impossible, the 82nd Airborne were called. They were the ones called upon when the missions needed to be completed. Their bravery had no match. I originally heard about this division from Lt. Col. Dave Grossman who is one of the most popular Law Enforcement trainers in the country. He tells this story at the end of his book, *On Combat*.

> During the Battle of the Bulge, the Nazi SS spearhead units had broken through

American lines in the Ardennes Forest in December of 1944, and the demoralized American units were fleeing in terror down the little roads coming out of the Ardennes Forest with the Nazis on their heels. My old unit, the 82nd Airborne Division, was brought out of reserve to help stop the enemy advance. The paratroopers of the 82nd marched day and night to establish blocking positions on the roads leading through the Ardennes Forest, and they had the mission, the authority and the responsibility to rally together the fleeing Americans and stop the Nazi advance. And that is exactly what they did.

There was an American tank, 30 tons of death, fleeing down one of the little roads leading through the forest. One lonely paratrooper stood beside the road. A photographer captured the image of this young man with hollow sunken eyes, a three-day growth of beard, an M-1 Garand in one hand, and a bazooka slung over his back. He raised his hand to stop the fleeing tank. After it had ground to a halt, the weary paratrooper looked up at the tank commander, and asked, "Buddy, are you looking for a safe place?"

"Yeah," the tank commander replied.

"Then park your tank behind me,
because I'm the 82nd Airborne, and this is
as far as the [Germans] are going [to get]."

These two men were faced with the same obstacle. The same seemingly overwhelming threat came at them both. One man's response was to run, flee from the problem, trying to escape its deadly grip. The other, facing the same fear as his companion, decided that he was not going to allow fear to control him. His response to his fear was to stand firm and face it. When fear pushed him, he pushed back.

As a guy, when I hear stories of such unwavering bravery, admiration instantly swells within me. Respect is earned by any individual who shows such courage. I long to have the same quality traits as this soldier had, to show fear that it has no power over me.

Allow me, however, to share my experience with fear that I had the week that I had become unemployed. I had a terrible nightmare one night. I tossed and turned for hours as a war raged inside my head. It was mentally devastating. I cannot specifically remember the dream and all that it contained but I do distinctly remember the feelings I had when I woke up. It was earlier than I normally wake up and nausea threatened to take the contents of my stomach and spread them all over the floor. As I got into the shower, exhaustion pummeled my body. The warm water did little to revive me as I lay in the bottom of the shower.

The tears would not come, dammed up behind my eyes. Never in my life have I ever seriously considered suicide but during that embattled morning, the thought came to my mind several times.

I felt alone. Fear haunted me. Uncertainty prophesied of my impending failure. My doubts taunted me and hurled insults at me. Death was the only way I could think of to end the barrage of lethal arrows that Fear, Doubt, Uncertainty and Loneliness were throwing at me. I had no idea how I was going to make it through the day, let alone the next few months. I remember my wife read the Bible to me as I collapsed onto our bed and then she prayed for me. I fell asleep to the sound of her voice and slept dreamlessly for the next few hours. That one was of the worst experiences I have ever had in my life.

When I went through the first few drafts of this book I had made a point to try to remain as positive as possible. There is enough negativity and depressing news out there, no need to add to it. This experience, however, was one that I wanted to share with you for a specific reason. If you have had a reaction remotely similar to mine, I know how lonely it felt. You are, however, not alone. Fear honors no treaty and does not accept any form of surrender. It is merciless in its assaults. You and I are not its only victims and we will not be its last ones either. Take heart though, there is light at the end of this tunnel. The only reason we sometimes can't see it is because Fear causes us to shut our eyes tight. Let us open our eyes together and we will see that Fear, though a worthy adversary, is conquerable.

LESSON

Although I had four tormentors that day, the mastermind behind it all was Fear. It often leads the charge against our will and our strength to move on. When the unknown in our future seems to spread across our path like a huge dark tarp, making us blind to the next few steps ahead, Fear invades our minds with the sole mission to destroy our will. Fear can cripple us and make us see things that are never there. Rationality and common sense flee the scene. Every small hill and little obstacle becomes an insurmountable problem that has no solution. Fear encourages us to give up and the temptation to give into its persuading is incredibly high.

When our futures are dark and we are not sure what we are going to be able to do tomorrow, we cannot allow fear to take control. Fear is what keeps us from trying. It does not want us to succeed. It wants us all to fail and see us curled up in the corner weeping in misery. Will we allow fear to do that to us?

CHALLENGE

We must take control of our minds right now. Do not let fear hold us back or cripple our motivation to move ahead with our lives. Fear only has as much power as we allow it to have. Our motivation and drive will poison fear. The more we cripple our fears, the stronger we become. We have the power to defeat the fear in our lives if only we take a stand.

There is a bright future for us out there. When we get there, we'll look back and see that it was fear that was blinding us, it was fear that made that valley seem deeper and darker than it actually was. Look ahead and do not look back. If we keep our eyes forward the darkness will fade. Do not give up hope. Fear brings an army against us. We are outnumbered and out gunned. Others around us are fleeing for their lives. We are broken and beat down. Our determination balances on the edge of a knife; stray just a little and it will break completely. Stand with me as we face Fear today. Let us say to it, "This is as far as you are going to get!"

CHAPTER ELEVEN

Stay Positive

TRIAL

I hate watching the news. I like to stay informed as much as I can, but I loathe national news pundits. There is no such thing to them as good news. We rarely hear about great, encouraging things happening around the world and in our own backyard. If 500 airplanes land safely at the airport, the only one we will ever know about is the one that crashed. Death, destruction, chaos, affairs, gossip and slander are seemingly the only newsworthy things they feel like reporting. They reek of negativity and gloom.

The world has too many pessimistic people. We all know somebody who is exceedingly negative. They often complain a lot and when something good comes along they disassemble it and complain about how bad it is. "If it sounds too good to be true," they say, "then it probably is." To them, the glass is always half empty and the other half is filled with backwash. They find ways to take the enjoyment out of the smallest pleasures in life. And they don't just stop at ruining their experiences. They feel compelled to open their stinking mouths and ruin those things for the rest of us. They often call themselves "realistic" in an attempt to disguise their negativity.

I had a pastor tell a story about a man he was mentoring and the pastor told this man to make of list of all the things he was thankful for. The next week, the pastor asked to see his list and the man handed him a blank piece of paper. The pastor said, "You couldn't find one thing to be thankful for? You're still breathing aren't you?" To which the man replied, "Yeah, but it is polluted air." I would never be like this man, I vowed. Then I started to pay attention.

I would have never noticed the negative voice inside me if I never started to listen for it. This negative voice that I recently discovered would speak up more often than I would have first guessed. And it was *loud!* Any good news I received, whether large or small, this voice would chime in and dismantle it and spin it in a negative light. Sometimes this voice inside my head would sneak out of my mouth. My wife, who also began to notice her own negative voice, would constantly point out how cynical I was being.

LESSON

Our negative voices often use the same words over and over again. It isn't very creative but it is very good at what is does. Words like "can't" and "impossible," "it'll never work," or "that's stupid" or "too good to be true" all come from our negative voice. It is the voice of fear and doubt, of rejection and failure. It often tells us that we will fail and gives us plenty of excuses to not try anything. If something good happens in our lives it is the voice that tends to ruin the moment by "bringing" us back to "reality." We all have this voice and we all let this voice speak too freely. Having this negative view on life greatly affects how we think and how we act. It affects how we deal with things in our lives and how we interact with the people we come into contact with.

No one knows where this voice comes from, but it doesn't deserve the power it has in our lives. Right now, our thoughts are the key ingredient to our success during this time. Allowing negative thoughts to control our minds is like putting dog poop into a wonderful batch of chocolate chip cookie dough. It ruins our thoughts and our views just like dog poop would ruin those cookies. It does not matter how much or how little gets into the batch, the entire product is unusable.

CHALLENGE

Do not ruin your mind with these thoughts. Take them captive and bind them up. Burn them, toss them, get rid of them anyway you can. We cannot afford to let this outlook ruin our future or our lives. Take special care this week to take every thought captive and decide if it is a negative or positive thought. Share with your spouse or with a friend about your goal to be more positive. Have them help you achieve this goal. My wife and I keep each other accountable and we have seen a huge difference in our lives.

When you start the practice of quieting this negative voice in your head, you'll begin to notice the negativity in others around as well. You will have the eyes to see how these kinds of thoughts and words really do *negatively* affect their lives. You begin to struggle in your desire to be around these kinds of people. They tend to suck the fun out of the little things in life that you enjoy. They make themselves miserable and they want you to join them in this misery. After all, misery loves company.

This is a life-changing process. Be purposeful in your life today and stay positive. A negative person has limited options and a higher rate of failure. A positive person has the world before him and can do anything he sets his mind to. Stay positive and you will get over this bump in the road. We have the power to accomplish whatever we set our minds too. It's time to be "realistic"; we *will* make it. There is hope, whether the nightly news says so or not.

CONCLUSION

This is Not the End

After I had lost my job I knew that the future was not at all hopeless. I knew that God would be looking out for me and my family and I knew that He had a plan for me. I had an optimistic view of the future and I thought I would be on my feet again in a matter of weeks with the world at my fingertips.

Instead, several months have passed and I find myself not on my feet like I had envisioned but on my knees in humility. God took me and brought me here because He had some very important lessons He needed to teach me. I have written those lessons for you here. I hope what I have learned through this time in my life has spoken to you in some way. I am a simple man with a simple life but who believes in an awesome God. This God took the time to teach me what He knew I needed to learn.

I told you this wasn't a religious book and it really isn't. This is just me being me. I cannot pretend to be something that I am not and my God has an active and real role in my life. That is who I am and that is how I must write to you today. However, as I come to the end of this book, I wanted to share one last thing about me that might help you understand *how* I was able to learn and apply these things in my life. This will take just a few minutes as I share more of my life with you. I strove to be completely honest with you throughout this whole book and I would fall short of achieving that goal if I left this important part out.

On first glance, these things that I wrote about are or can be extremely difficult to change in our lives. In the first lesson I spoke about knowing and acknowledging that there is a higher power and that I call that power God. For me, as I reflect on these lessons, I know beyond any shadow of a doubt that I would have never learned them if God didn't play a very active role in my life. I have a personal relationship with Jesus Christ, who I believe is my personal Savior. It is because of my belief that I was able to learn and, more importantly, apply the things that I was taught. It was because of this relationship that I was able to overcome fear and doubt. Jesus is the reason I have hope for the future and the reason I felt I must share that with you. In the Bible it says in 1 Peter 3:15 for me to "always [be] prepared to make a defense to anyone who asks you for a reason for the hope that is in you; yet do it with gentleness and respect,". I would not have made it through those first dark days if it wasn't for Jesus being by my side. And I wouldn't be completely honest with you if I did not admit that.

I share these things with you with the goal being only to show you *how* I was able to accomplish all these things that have happened to me. The *reason* I did not give into the temptation to take my life, the *reason* my wife and I have continued to grow stronger in our relationship, the *reason* I can move boldly into the future, the *reason* I had the courage to share all this with you is *because* of Jesus the Christ and the amazing changes he has brought into my life. The reason I have made it this far and can continue on is summed up in Philippians 4:12-13:

> "I know how to be brought low, and I know how to abound. In any and every circumstance, I have learned the secret of facing plenty and hunger, abundance and need. *I can do all things through him who strengthens me.*" (ESV, emphasis mine)

This is the reason, friends. This is the only reason I can do what I write about here. This task is not impossible nor these challenges insurmountable with Jesus in your life.

I want to thank you for allowing me to share my story with you. I know my story is not one that is unique. The goal of this little book was to encourage those of you who find themselves at an uncertain time in their life and to share what I have learned about being unemployed. Some of the lessons I thought I already knew. Others I never knew I needed to learn. I have grown as a person over the past few months and it had everything to do with the lessons written here. And as I look back over these experiences, I don't think I would change how things happened if I were given that choice. I do not know when my life's circumstances will change nor do I know when things will turn around for you. I don't know when the economy will flip over and begin to grow again. I don't know a lot of things about the future. I, however, would never trade these lessons I learned for anything.

Things will get better for you and your family. Things will get better for this country. I just don't know when. Your future is bright and all you have to do is believe that. I hope you can see as you are living this life of ups and downs that you have the opportunity to learn these vital lessons. What we take in now, the lessons we learn during the tough times are the things that stay with us for the rest of our lives. They are embedded into our self-conscious and become a part of who we are as human beings.

I hope you see the value in these lessons written here for you. This is not an in-depth look by any means and some of you will learn even more lessons than what I have learned. Some of you will spend most of this season learning one or two of them on a deeper level. When this season is over I know I will look back and see this as the turning point in my life. I will see this as the point where I grew the most as a person. This isn't the end for me and I know that. This isn't the end for you either. Be mindful of the teachings life is giving you right now. We all have a lot to learn. We will make it! Good luck to you, my friend, and here's to your success!

Look for my fan page on

facebook.

.